Contents

Any words appearing in the text in bold, **like this**, are explained in the Glossary.

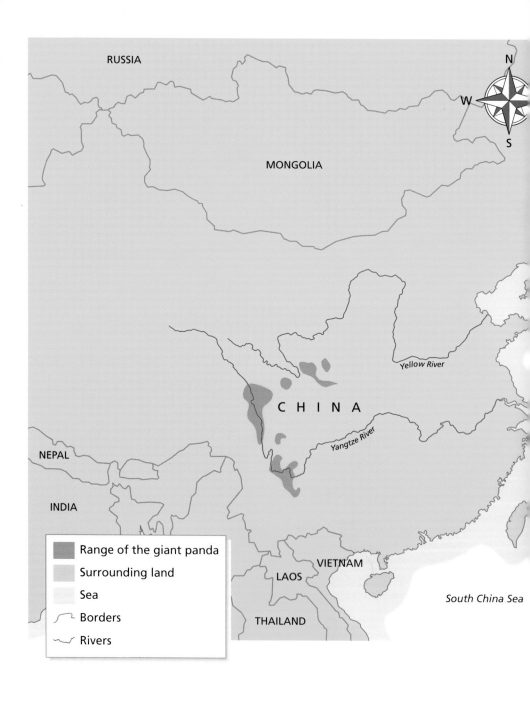

Giant Pandas

By Duncan Scheff

Raintree

ANIMALS OF THE RAINFOREST

www.raintreepublishers.co.uk

Visit our website to find out more information about Raintree books.

To order:
- ☎ Phone 44 (0) 1865 888112
- 🖹 Send a fax to 44 (0) 1865 314091
- 🖳 Visit the Raintree Bookshop at www.raintreepublishers.co.uk to browse our catalogue and order online.

First published in Great Britain by Raintree Publishers, Halley Court, Jordan Hill, Oxford, OX2 8EJ, part of Harcourt Education.
Raintree is a registered trademark of Harcourt Education Ltd.

Originated by Dot Gradations
Printed and bound in China by South China Printing

ISBN 1 844 21128 2
07 06 05 04 03
10 9 8 7 6 5 4 3 2 1

British Library Cataloguing in Publication Data
Scheff, Duncan
1. Giant panda – Juvenile literature
2. Rainforest ecology – Juvenile literature
599.7'89
A catalogue for this book is available from the British Library.

Acknowledgements
The publishers would like to thank the following for permission to reproduce photographs:
Root Resources/Kenneth Fink, pp. **14, 16, 28–29**; Alan Nelson, p. **22**; Visuals Unlimited; Fritz Polking, pp. **1, 12**; Images International, p. **6**; Bill Kamin, pp. **8, 18**; Mark Newman, p. **24**; Arthur Morris, p. **26**; Wildlife Conservation Society, headquartered at the Bronx Zoo/Bill Meng, pp. **11, 21**; NHPA, pp. **5, 23, 27**.

Cover photograph reproduced with permission of Getty images/Taxi

A quick look at giant pandas

What do giant pandas look like?

Giant pandas are like large bears. They are covered in thick fur with black and white markings. Giant pandas have heavy bodies and round heads. They also have small white tails.

Where do giant pandas live?

Giant pandas live mainly in the forest-covered mountains of central China. Most of them live in wildlife reserves protected by China's government. The two main reserves are the Wanglang Reserve and the Wolong Reserve.

What do giant pandas eat?

Pandas eat mostly **bamboo**. They only rarely eat meat that they find.

This giant panda is climbing a bamboo tree in China's rainforest.

Giant pandas in the rainforest

Giant pandas are black and white. Some scientists think pandas are related to bears. Other scientists think they are related to raccoons. Pandas are mammals. A mammal is a warm-blooded animal with a backbone. Warm-blooded animals have a body temperature that stays the same, no matter what the air temperature is. The females give birth to live young and feed them milk from their bodies.

The scientific name for the giant panda is *Ailuropoda Melanoleuca*. The name means 'black and white cat-foot'. The panda has a long wristbone with an extra 'thumb'.

Wild giant pandas live only in China. There are more than 30 Chinese names for the panda. The most common name is *da xiongmao*, which means 'large bear-cat'.

> **This panda is resting on the floor of the forest.**

Where do giant pandas live?

Once, pandas lived throughout large areas of China. Many parts of the forests were cut down to make houses for people. Today, pandas live in the wet mountain forests of central China. Most pandas live in the Chinese provinces of Sichuan, Gansu and Shaanxi.

Pandas need to eat a plant called bamboo to live. Bamboo is a tree-like grass. It has a strong, woody stem. Pandas live in forests where bamboo grows.

The bamboo that pandas eat grows in mountain areas 2600 to 3050 metres above sea level. Sea level is the average level of the ocean's water. Weather in the mountains changes depending on their height above sea level. Higher places are cooler than lower places. Tall mountain peaks may even receive some snowfall during summer.

Bamboo forests are very wet because they receive a lot of rainfall. The air is usually moist. Sometimes clouds cover the forests for days at a time.

Almost all of the world's wild pandas live in the Wanglang Reserve and the Wolong Reserve in China. A reserve is a place where plants and animals can live safely. The Chinese government protects pandas in these places. People are not allowed to cut down trees or to farm land in reserves. The reserves are located in the Min Mountains and the Qionglai Mountains.

What do giant pandas look like?

Giant pandas look like large bears with round heads and heavy bodies. Males are longer and heavier than females. Most pandas are from 1.5 to 1.8 metres long. Adult giant pandas usually weigh between 75 and 110 kilograms. The largest panda ever found weighed 181 kilograms.

Giant pandas have special black and white markings on their fur. Their legs, feet and ears are black. Their bodies and heads are white. Black fur surrounds their eyes. Pandas also have small black or white bushy tails.

Scientists are not sure why pandas have such an unusual colouring. It is easy to spot a panda in summer. But scientists think the colours may **camouflage** the panda in winter. Camouflage is special colours, shapes and patterns that help an animal blend in with its surroundings. The black and white colours may help the panda blend in with the black rocks and tree trunks and white snow.

Panda fur is thick and stiff. It keeps the panda warm during cold, winter weather.

You can see the thick fur on this panda. It helps keep the animal warm.

The fur is also coated with oil from the panda's body. The oil seals in the panda's heat. It also helps the panda keep dry. The air in the panda's **habitat** is almost always moist with water. A habitat is a place where an animal or plant usually lives. The oil stops the water from soaking into the fur. Instead, the water slides off the panda's fur.

This panda is settling down for a rest in an area of its home range.

Home ranges

Pandas spend most of their time alone. Only mother pandas and their young live together. The only other time pandas gather is during the mating season.

Each adult panda has its own home range. A home range is a place where an animal normally lives and searches for food. These areas are from 4 to 10 square kilometres (1.5 to 4 square miles). Males often have larger ranges than females. If lots of pandas live in one area, the edges of two pandas' ranges sometimes overlap. But two pandas will not go into the overlapping area at the same time.

Each panda has its own special scent. Pandas can tell the difference between each other's scent. By sniffing scents, pandas can tell which other pandas have been in the area. The scent also reveals a panda's size and whether or not it is ready to mate.

A panda marks its home range with its scent. It rubs special body parts against trees to leave its scent mark. This scent tells other pandas to stay out of the home range.

Some of a panda's home range may include water. Pandas are excellent swimmers. They may swim in rivers to move to different parts of their home range. Clumps of bamboo trees may be growing on different sides of a river. Once a panda has eaten bamboo from one side of the river, it needs to move to the other side of the river to eat the bamboo that grows there.

This panda is eating bamboo that it has found.

What giant pandas eat

Pandas are **omnivores**. This means that they eat both plants and meat. Pandas may eat meat from dead animals they find. But bamboo makes up 99 per cent of a panda's diet.

Pandas eat mainly two types of bamboo – umbrella bamboo and arrow bamboo. Umbrella bamboo is the main source of panda food. This thick bamboo grows in bunches on low mountain slopes. Some umbrella bamboo can grow up to 5 metres tall.

Arrow bamboo grows higher on mountain slopes than umbrella bamboo does. It grows in very thick bunches. The plants are thinner and shorter than umbrella bamboo plants. The average height of arrow bamboo is 1.4 metres.

Pandas spend most of their days
eating bamboo.

Finding food and eating

Pandas must eat a great deal of food to stay
alive. Every day, they eat between 10 and
20 kilograms of bamboo.

Pandas spend twelve hours or more every day
eating. They must spend this time eating
because their body does not digest plants well.

Digest means to break down food in the stomach so the body can use it. Pandas cannot digest the cell walls of bamboo. A cell is a tiny part of an animal or plant. The cell walls of bamboo contain more energy than the inside of the cell. Pandas must eat a lot of bamboo to get the energy they need from inside the bamboo plant cells.

Pandas eat different parts of bamboo plants at different times of the year. They eat whatever parts of bamboo they can find each season. From November to March, pandas eat growing stems and leaves called shoots. They eat old stems from April to June. During July to October, they eat mostly leaves.

Pandas hold bamboo stems in their front feet to eat. They can do this because they have special 'thumbs'. They are not thumbs like people have, but short, padded growths on their wristbones. Pandas use them to grasp objects.

Pandas have strong jaw muscles to help them chew through the bamboo. Sharp front teeth called **canines** cut through the woody stems. Large, flat teeth called **molars** crush and grind the bamboo. A panda's stomach has a thick lining to protect it from sharp pieces of bamboo.

Pandas come together only during the mating season. Otherwise, they live alone.

A giant panda's life cycle

Pandas begin mating when they are about six years old. They mate only during their mating season each spring.

Female pandas mark their ranges with a special scent when they are ready to mate. Males can smell this scent a long way away. Females may also roar loudly to call male pandas.

Male pandas enter a female's range to mate. A male panda that finds a mate may also roar loudly. Some males even climb to the top of a tree to roar. The sound tells other male pandas to stay away.

Sometimes, two males arrive to mate with a female at the same time. The two males may then fight for the female. The male that wins the fight will mate with the female.

Young

After mating, the female finds or builds a den. Common places for dens are rocky caves, thick growths of bamboo and hollow tree trunks.

Five months after mating, the female goes into her den and gives birth. Newborn pandas are called cubs. She may give birth to one, two or three cubs. She will usually raise only the first cub. Raising more than one cub is very hard and takes a lot of food and energy. The mother often leaves the other cubs to die.

A newborn panda only weighs about 100 grams. It has no fur and no teeth. Its eyes are closed. The mother licks the newborn cub clean. She then feeds it milk from her body. This is called **nursing**.

The mother stays with the cub at all times to keep it safe from **predators**. A predator is an animal that hunts other animals for food. In the first few months, the pandas rarely leave the den. Young pandas often cry loudly. This sound may attract predators. If they do leave the den, the mother carries the cub in her mouth.

After two months, cubs have fur and teeth and can see. At five months, young pandas can

This panda cub is old enough to climb trees on its own.

move around easily. They often roll on the ground and climb on to their mothers. Cubs stop nursing and begin eating bamboo at about twelve months old.

A cub stays with its mother for about two years. Then it leaves to find its own home range. Pandas live for up to 20 years in the wild. Pandas in zoos may live for up to 30 years.

This panda has stopped to eat because it has found a clump of bamboo.

 The giant panda is one of the most endangered species in the world. When the World Wide Fund for Nature formed in 1961, it chose the giant panda to be its symbol. The WWF has spent millions of pounds on panda conservation in China. It is helping the Chinese to create new reserves for giant pandas and to reduce the illegal hunting of pandas. It is also helping to educate the public about pandas and show people how they can live without destroying the bamboo forest where the pandas live.

A panda's day

Pandas are active for about fifteen hours each day, mostly in the early morning and evening. Pandas spend much of the day moving around their home range. They climb trees and eat. They then move on to find another patch of bamboo. During the day, pandas take several naps lasting two to four hours each. They usually find a tree or rock to lean against when they sleep.

Pandas also spend some time **grooming** their fur. They lick themselves to stay clean.

Giant pandas are in danger because bamboo is being cut down.

The future of giant pandas

Giant pandas are endangered. This means that they are in danger of dying out. Scientists think that the number of pandas has halved since the 1960s. Today, only about 1000 wild pandas are left in China.

Other animals do not hunt adult pandas. Pandas are in danger because their habitat is disappearing. Many bamboo forests have been cut down and turned into farms. Without their homes or enough to eat, pandas cannot survive.

The way bamboo grows puts pandas in danger too. Bamboo has a long growth cycle. All the bamboo plants in one place start growing at the same time and die at the same time. When there was more forest, pandas moved to a new area at the end of a bamboo cycle. Today, there is not enough forest for pandas to do this.

▲ **Pandas cannot survive without enough bamboo to eat.**

What will happen to pandas?

Many people are working to save pandas. Scientists study pandas and how they live. They hope this information will help them understand how to keep pandas safe and healthy.

The Chinese government is also trying to save pandas. It has set up several wildlife reserves for

In 1974, China gave the UK two pandas as a gift. The pandas were called Chia-Chia and Ching-Ching. They lived at London Zoo and were one of the major attractions for over ten years. Unfortunately, no pandas live in London Zoo at the moment.

pandas and has passed laws against hunting or catching pandas. Some people use panda body parts as medicine. Now it is illegal for people to take pandas out of the country. The government will not sell the animals either.

Scientists want to help pandas find bamboo. They set aside strips of undisturbed land between reserves called **corridors**. The corridors allow pandas to move from one reserve to another. This may help pandas stay alive at the end of a bamboo cycle. They can move to another area to find food. Scientists also want to plant new bamboo. This bamboo will be on a different cycle to the bamboo that already exists.

Scientists do not know if there are enough pandas and land left to allow the animals to survive. But people will keep working to save the giant panda from becoming **extinct**.

round head
see pages 5, 10

ears
see page 10

strong jaws
see page 17

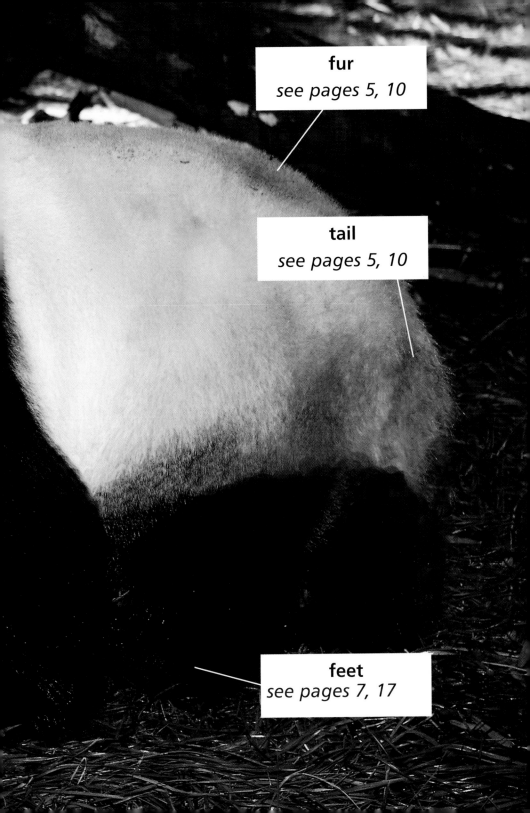

fur
see pages 5, 10

tail
see pages 5, 10

feet
see pages 7, 17

Glossary

bamboo tree-like grass with a wood-like stem

camouflage colours, shapes and patterns that help an animal or plant blend in with the things around it

canine sharp front tooth

corridor thin strip of undisturbed land that connects two wildlife reserves

extinct when all of one kind of animal has died out

grooming when an animal cleans itself or another animal's body

habitat surroundings that an animal or plant needs to survive

molar flat back tooth used to crush and grind food

nursing when a mother feeds her young the milk made inside her body

omnivore animal that eats both plants and animals

predator animal that hunts other animals for food

Internet sites

London Zoo
www.londonzoo.co.uk

World Wide Fund for Nature (WWF)
www.panda.org

Useful address

WWF – UK
Panda House, Weyside Park
Godalming, Surrey
GU7 1XR

Book to read

Theodorou, Rod. *Animals in Danger: Giant Panda.* Heinemann Library, Oxford, 2001

Index